Originally published May 2021
Second edition published February 2023
Third edition published January 2024

Contents

Glossary

Privatisation

the transfer from public or government control or ownership to private ownership.

The Mandem

originates from Caribbean English, combining the words 'man' and 'them', and has been adopted in Multicultural London English. It refers to a diverse group of individuals, predominantly but not exclusively comprising racialised and/or working-class individuals.

The Ends

refers to an area, neighborhood, city, or space, often encompassing social housing estates that are owned by the state or public sector organizations.

Zero Sum Game

the Mandem wins and the Ends loses; or the Ends wins and the Mandem loses.

Non-Zero Sum Game

the Mandem wins and the Ends wins; a win-win situation.

Social Housing

housing which provides affordable rent levels, secure tenancies and is owned by a social landlord.

Commodity

a product of value that can be traded, bought, or sold.

Public Sector

a group of organisations that are usually owned and/or operated by government.

Local Authority

a devolved public administration responsible for public functions such as social care, education, waste and housing.

Housing Association

a not-for-profit organisation providing low-cost rental housing for social housing tenants. Although considered "private" entities, they are regulated by the public sector.

Private Sector (Developers)

a group of for-profit organisations that are usually owned and/or operated by private entities.

Gentrification

the process in which a space or city experiences a change that displaces existing inhabitants (people and businesses) and replaces them with wealthier newcomers.

The Right to the City

right to change and reinvent the city after one's desire.

Amenity

a desirable or useful feature of a building or place (e.g. local parks, transportation links, cultural venues)

Capitalism

an economic and political system in which a nation's trade and industries are controlled by private for-profit organisations, rather than by the public sector.

Austerity

the conditions a population experiences as a result of reduced public spending, justified by "reducing luxuries" and subjectively non-essential expenditures.

Tenant

an individual who occupies a property that they rent from a landlord, over a specified duration of time.

Leasehold

the temporary ownership of a property over a predetermined duration. Ownership of a leased property reverts to the freeholder once the duration of a lease has ended. Costs associated with a lease include ground rent, services charges and/or any other landlord charges.

Service Charge

the costs charged by landlords to cover the cost of services to leased premises. e.g. general maintenance, repairs, insurance etc.

Freehold

the absolute ownership of land or property. A freeholder is the owner of the freehold (aka landlord).

Ground Rent

a payment made by a leaseholder to their landlord for occupying space under their freehold.

Solicitor

a legal practitioner that deals with legal matters.

Property Management Company

an organisation that can own and manage a residential building.

Shareholder

an individual who owns a share of a company, otherwise known as equity in a company. Shareholders are essentially the owners of a company.

Articles of Association

the written rules on running a company agreed by the shareholders. A document which defines the responsibilities of members and the nature of the company.

Building Surveyor

a professional that advises their clients on the design, construction, valuation, maintenance and repair of buildings. They survey buildings and report findings to the client, providing them with recommendations.

Leaseback(s)

a legal agreement by which a new owner of a building provides the previous owner a leasehold on dwelling(s) of the building.

Outsourcing

bringing in external individuals/ companies to deliver a service and/ or goods.

Insourcing

using in-house individuals/ companies to deliver a service and/ or goods.

Asset Management

the management of an asset's ("building") operations and maintenance.

Revenue

the net income of an asset after expenses.

Building Maintenance

the process of keeping a building at optimum efficiency and at a good aesthetic.

Renovations

works undertaken to return an asset to a good or acceptable level of repair.

Placemaking

the design and planning decisions, that lead to creating an inclusive and functional place.

Hear

Chapter One

me out

This was written for the Mandem. The "*Mandem*" being: the aunties, the uncles, the young bucks, the girls, the guys, the sisters, the akhis, the preachers and the sinners. Anyone and everyone that makes up our inner-city communities. Hear me out for a second...

The Mandem have been active. Against all odds our people are really out here doing bits. And it's oh so sweet to see.

When we do business, we make a pretty penny;
when we make music, we make it sound jumpy;
when we dress up, the whole country follows suit;
and when we speak, we make headlines.

We've been setting up shop across the country and have been dictating the direction of popular culture for a hot minute now. And it's no fluke either, our successes aren't accidental. It's in our nature to pioneer movements, to take the initiative and disrupting the status quo.

And still, the Mandem face prejudice. We are still continuously hungry. We are still maliciously ill-informed. We are still irrationally feared. We are still unreasonably hated. We are still economically excluded. And we are still labelled as monsters. Our forefathers protested and campaigned against this prejudice decades ago, and we still find ourselves protesting and campaigning against the very same prejudice decades later. At every election and referendum, the Mandem are the first to feel the effects of policy, due to our dependency on the state. We are constantly at the mercy of the ballot. This puts us at a permanent disadvantage, as it is near impossible to create a nurturing and functional community when operating under this form of political turbulence.

So, what is the remedy to our affliction? And, how do we utilise our strengths to our advantage?

The answer: **we privatise the Mandem.**

Privatisation /prʌɪvətʌɪˈzeɪʃ(ə)n/

noun: the transfer from public or government control or ownership to private ownership.

To *privatise the Mandem* is to take control of our situation, to become independent of the countless variables that affect our lives. Privatisation grants us a seat at tables where important political decisions are made, and entitles us to a vote in the forums that shape the nation. It denationalises our communities, and gives us sovereignty and agency. It redistributes power into our communities and permits us to set our own economic agenda; an agenda that's informed by our own social needs.

This solution requires heavy endorsement and large-scale coordination from our communities. It also calls for internal investment from the Mandem, which is much easier said than done. How do you mobilise a community of individuals who have been in survival mode for years? To privatise the Mandem is no small feat, it's a big ask. The current condition of our communities doesn't leave a lot of room for this form of intervention. And why even privatise? The Mandem have had a pretty turbulent relationship with the Ends. Some of us have lost people to the soil because of the Ends, some of us have lost people to the system because of the Ends, some of us suffer from trauma because of the Ends. The strenuous relationship we have with the Ends can leave little incentive for investing, improving and developing such an environment.

Understandably it may seem counterproductive to even consider *privatising* a place that brings so much grief to its residents. The dynamic between the Mandem and the Ends has established an enduring belief that *'prosperity'* and *'the Ends'* are an oxymoron, creating what's known as a zero-sum game— either the Mandem win and the Ends lose, or the Ends win and the Mandem lose.

Status Quo
'Zero Sum Game'

The
Mandem
Win

The
Ends
Win

To privatise is to challenge this belief. To encourage the consumption of our own domestic products, and to keep money circulating within the Ends. To privatise is to promote the investment and retention of homegrown talent, preventing a brain drain— as is usually experienced in the Ends.

Privatisation is a non-zero sum game where an individual's success is a contributor to the success of the collective. Currently, 'success' in the Ends is a zero-sum game. To privatise would mean to collectively redefine what 'success' means to the Mandem.

Privatisation
'Non-Zero Sum Game'

To privatise the Mandem, we have to change the game and you can't privatise without the 'power' to do so. There are three forms of power that are required for privatisation, with the first being...

1) The ability to '*influence*'

In recent years, numerous members of our community have been representing us on practically every single platform of communication. The Mandem are on all the screens; from international silver screens to primetime television. From your BBC's to your ITV's. Pirate radio to national radio. You'll find us in Hollywood, and you'll find us on YouTube. We've been voicing our opinions and sharing new perspectives on subject matters through literature, podcasting and film-making.

And when it comes to accolades in these fields— we're cleaning up. There's not one channel of communication the Mandem are not dominating. We create the slanguage and directly influence the way the nation communicates with each other. Our culture has led the fashion and music industry for decades now. The Mandem are independently charting with ease nowadays. And every time we speak, we make the papers. The nation listens to us attentively.

Naturally with every channel of influence, there's the opportunity to earn some cash. Which leads us nicely to...

2) The generation of 'capital'

The Wu Tang Clan said it best: "*cash rules everything around me*". A common trait that all the Mandem share, is that we're all bred hustlers— a circumstance of our upbringing. We're society's go-getters. Generating capital? That's second nature.

When you think of music, who's taking up the most space on the charts? When you think of sports, who's holding all the belts, trophies, and medals? When you think of fashion, who is everyone trying to dress like? The common denominator here, is that the Mandem are dominating. And when you factor in all the restaurants, media platforms and businesses that the Mandem have constructed, there's no choice but to recognise the hustle.

The relationship between influence and capital is symbiotic, as they both drive each other. Audiences are naturally inclined to support individuals or groups leading in their discipline— and this support can subsequently be translated into currency.

The Mandem are fluent in influencing audiences and capital generation, but it's the third form of power that is the most important for privatisation. And it's a form of power that is lacking in the Ends...

3) The acquisition of *'property'*

From being posted on a corner of South Central LA with the Rollin' 60s, to owning that very same corner Ermias Joseph Asghedom, better known as Nipsey Hussle, understood the value of property and the power it provides communities. Properties are the skeletal frames that house enterprise, family, creativity and, most importantly agency.

Privatisation isn't dependent on whether we have the ability to invest in property, it's dependent on *where* we choose to invest...

Brown Diamonds

Chapter Two

& Lobsters

The Ends are almost exclusively defined as an area of social housing where the landlord is either a local authority or a housing association (not-for-profit organisations offering housing to low-income communities). In the majority of cases, residents are charged a weekly or monthly rent which is often paid for through government welfare. This dependency on the state means that the Ends is always at the mercy of the ballot box. With every passing election, the newly-elected Government's housing and welfare policies directly impact our own housing and welfare services.

The purchase of property is where the zero-sum game is largely exhibited. Through no fault of our own, it's become increasingly difficult to purchase a house. An individual may purchase property out of the Ends and it'll be cheaper, but your friends, family and community would be out of reach. Couple that with the added complexity of being a migrant individual living outside of the safety of the Ends, and things get even more difficult.

You could buy property inside the Ends and you'll still be surrounded by everyone you love, but the hood politics don't stop when you get a mortgage. Furthermore, you'd likely be forking out hundreds of thousands of pounds on a lease which would only grant you tenancy for a limited number of years. Plus, it's difficult justifying the purchase of a flat in a poorly maintained area with a less than aesthetic backdrop.

And then, there's the potential to falling victim to...

"... the process of renewal and rebuilding, accompanying the influx of middle-class or affluent people into deteriorating areas that often displaces poorer residents."

– Furious Styles, Boyz n the Hood[1] (1991)

Better known as, gentrification. These past couple decades have seen the landscape of the Ends changing dramatically. Its practise can be seen prominently in London Boroughs of Brent, Camden, Islington, Southwark, Hackney etc. but its not limited to London— it is a nationwide dilemma. Social housing blocks are being replaced with glossy gated-communities, complete with futuristic living facilities, logos and colour palettes to market a glamourous 'inner-city living' lifestyle experience at our expense. You'd have thought that they were specifically out to uproot us, but the reality is that it's a lot more complicated than that; we're collateral damage in an otherwise perfect storm.

Reduction of central government funding over the last decade has resulted in widespread changes in housing, including:

(i) expectations on local authorities to generate funds independently, in the absence of support from central government,

(ii) reduction of welfare for working-class communities in the Ends, and

(iii) social housing responsibilities becoming a drain on local authority resources.

The sale of land is one of many commercial decisions local authorities make in order to fill the funding gap left by austerity, which in turn has invited the private sector into spaces once reserved for social housing. The private sector isn't best suited to cater for social housing tenants as the private sector's economic model is designed to generate as much money as possible— and providing social housing is a drain on that model. Additionally, when private sector developers build full market value properties adjacent to the Ends, the Mandem are subsequently priced out (a form of indirect displacement).

So... what do private sector developers see that we don't see? Why would they look to purchase land that our communities try so hard to get away from?

From as early as the 16th Century and as late as the 20th Century, lobsters were known as the 'poor man's protein'. An essayist in 1876, once wrote that: "*Lobster shells about a house are looked upon as signs of poverty and degradation*". Fast forward to today, someone saw value in lobsters and decided to mark up the price. As a result, lobster has become a delicacy for the posh and the rich.

Similarly, a more recent phenomenon would be the rise of the brown diamond, also known as the 'chocolate diamond' (trademarked by the Le Vian group). These diamonds are some of the least valuable and most commonly mined diamonds in the market.

Due to their high opacity and lack of shine, they were historically used for industrial purposes e.g. creating diamond drill bits for construction equipment. But similar to the story of the lobster, a name change and a marketing campaign was all it took for this otherwise worthless diamond to become commercially successful.

Through the eyes of the average man, the Ends is nothing to be desired, but the 'undesirable' can look very different when viewed through the lens of a private developer:

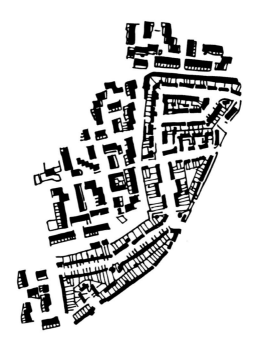

St. Raphael's estate
London Borough of Brent, NW10

- Zone 3 fare zone on the TfL network
- Bakerloo, Metropolitan, Overground and Jubilee line stations within two-mile radius
- Chiltern Railway station within two-mile radius
- River Brent flows through the length of the estate, accompanied by mile long green space
- Adjacent to the North Circular Road (A406)
- Four Primary schools within a two-mile radius
- Five-minute drive or 15-minute walk to Wembley National Stadium
- Numerous local amenities such as IKEA, Tesco, BAPS Swaminarayan Temple and more

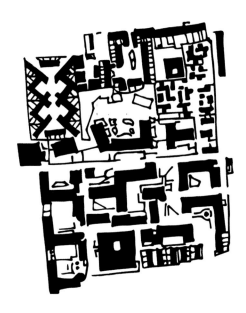

Broadwater Farm estate
London Borough of Haringey, N17

- Zone 3 fare zone on the TfL network
- Piccadilly, Overground and Victoria line stations within two-mile radius
- Greater Anglia, Great Northern, Stansted Express and Thameslink stations within two-mile radius
- Adjacent to the Lordship Recreational Grounds, Bruce Castle Park and Downhills Park
- 30-minute walk or 10-minute drive to the River Lea and Walthamstow Reservoirs
- 10-minute drive to the North Circular Road (A406)
- 10 Primary schools within a one-mile radius
- Six-minute drive or 25-minute walk to Tottenham Hotspur Stadium
- Numerous local amenities

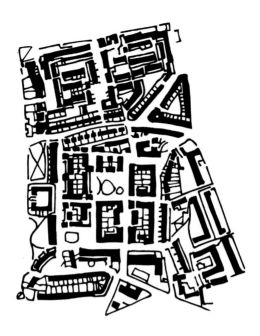

Angell Town estate
London Borough of Lambeth, SW9

- Zone 2 fare zone on the TfL network
- Overground, Northern and Victoria line stations within two-mile radius
- South Eastern and Thameslink stations within two-mile radius
- Within one-mile radius of Slade Gardens, Max Roach Park and Myatt's Fields Park
- Clapham Common Park within two-mile radius
- 30-minute walk or eight minute drive to the River Thames
- 10-minute drive to the South Circular Road (A205)
- 14 Primary schools within a two-mile radius
- Four-minute drive or 20-minute walk to The Oval Cricket Grounds
- Numerous local amenities such as O2 Academy Brixton, Windmill Brixton, Electric Brixton and more

North Peckham estates
London Borough of Southwark, SE15

- Zone 2 fare zone on the TfL network
- Overground line stations within two-mile radius
- Southern, South Eastern and Thameslink stations within two-mile radius
- Within one-mile radius of Burgess Park and Surrey Linear Canal Park
- Numerous green spaces within two-mile radius, such as Brunswick Park, Lucas Gardens, Sceaux Gardens, Central Venture Park, Calypso Gardens, Camberwell Green etc.
- 15-minute drive to the River Thames
- 17-minute drive to the South Circular Road (A205)
- 18 local schools within a two-mile radius, as well as University of Arts London and Kings College London
- 12-minute drive to The Oval Cricket Grounds
- Numerous local amenities such as The Feminist Library, Peckham Library, Peckham High Street, Southwark Tigers Rugby Club and more

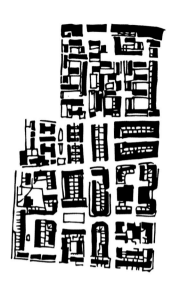

Holly Street estate
London Borough of Hackney, E8

- Zone 2 fare zone on the TfL network
- Overground line stations within two-mile radius
- Greater Anglia station within two-mile radius
- Numerous green spaces within two-mile radius, such as Stonebridge Gardens, De Beauvoir Square and Dalston Eastern Curve Garden
- Nine minute walk to the London Fields, 11-minute walk to Haggerston Park and 25-minute walk to Victoria Park
- 15-minute drive into City of London
- 17 local schools within a two-mile radius
- 15-minute drive to Queen Elizabeth Olympic Park, West Ham United Stadium and the River Lea
- Local amenities include Dalston Junction, London Fields Lido, Shoreditch, V&A Museum of Childhood and numerous pubs/clubs

The story of the Ends is not too different to the story of brown diamonds and lobsters— our blocks too, are a commodity. And the price is goin' up.

Love

Chapter Three

Thyself

'*Privatising*' may seem a tad bit excessive. But when considering the trajectory and pace of changes being made in our urban spaces, it increasingly becomes the only way we can preserve our communities and the spaces they occupy. So, how did we reach this point? Why does privatisation seem like the only viable method of preservation? Let's set the scene...

As a result of a decade long austerity campaign initiated by the 2010 Conservative and Liberal Democrat coalition government,[2] local authorities have been strapped for cash.[3,4] Everything from housing, health, policing and public services had their budgets slashed.[5]

Running concurrently, is the UK Housing Crisis. The UK has been experiencing a chronic shortage in housing, continually failing to meet housing demand. As such, pressure has been mounting for the market to quickly produce enough housing to meet housing demand. Social housing forms part of the housing demand in the UK, and can be delivered through three means:

Social Housing Delivered via the Public Sector

The overall supply of public sector-owned social housing has been steadily decreasing since the early 1980s.[6,7] This decline in social housing stock is largely credited to the *Right to Buy* legislation first introduced in 1980, which allowed social housing tenants to purchase the homes they were occupying from local authorities at a discounted rate. The decline in social housing stock didn't necessarily pose an issue. After all, the more economically active individuals there are in a nation's economy, the healthier the economy. Therefore, allowing social housing tenants to become homeowners and to finally get on the property ladder, directly increased their economic activity, and boosted the overall health of the economy. With government-subsidised grants and continuous house-building, public sector budgets were regularly replenished and public sector-owned social housing stock were maintained at healthy levels.

Then came the 2007/08 Global Financial Crisis, which produced the then-Prime Minister's Affordable Homes Programme which dramatically reduced government-subsidised grants for housing.[8] To fill the funding gap created by the reduction, local authorities were left with no choice but to borrow funds from HM Treasury. The aforementioned *Right to Buy* legislation left local authorities with reduced housing stock to borrow against, resulting in astronomical interest rates imposed on loans by the treasury. Operating under these conditions had made borrowing from HM Treasury an unviable option.[9,10]

Still expected to build quickly enough to meet housing demand— whilst spending minimally due to the constraints of austerity, local authorities end up compensating for these gaps in funding by compromising on design, affordability and quality when building new homes. Social housing is often a drain on local authority resources, as the majority of social tenants have their rent partially or fully covered by government welfare. Redeveloping existing social housing areas and compromising on the affordability of the newly developed homes reduces the number of social tenants. This reduces the amount of government welfare a local authority must spend, which in turn supports closing the funding gap created by austerity measures implemented by the central government.

Social Housing Delivered via the Private Sector

'*Social housing*' and the '*private sector*' are two opposing terms. The first adopts a primarily not-for-profit model in order to provide tenancies with affordable low rents, whereas the latter adopts a for-profit model aiming to make as much money as possible.

In recent years, rather than bearing the brunt of the costs associated with house-building, local authorities are utilising legislative tools which permit them to use the private sector to meet their house-building targets. Legislative tools such as *Section 106 of the Town and Country Planning Act 1990*, allow the public sector to harvest a percentage of the housing built by the private sector. This undoubtedly has its flaws, as the private sector's economic model is for-profit and providing social housing is a drain on that model.

Loopholes such as '*viability assessments*' are regularly exploited in order to reduce the amount of houses destined for handover to the public sector.[11] The less houses handed over to the public sector, the more housing stock becomes available for profit generating private rent. Furthermore, housing that eventually gets handed over to the public sector is usually of sub-standard quality. This malpractice is widely adopted by the private sector in order to save on material costs and maximise profits.[12,13]

It's also common practice that homes, destined for transfer to the public sector and intended for social housing tenancies, are segregated from private tenants who pay full market rent rates. Examples of these forms of separation include denying social housing tenants access to communal gardens and/or providing social housing tenants separate entrances from private renters, callously dubbed "*poor doors*".[14–16] Moreover, the private sector publicly admits that it doesn't think that the responsibility of social housing should fall on them.[17]

Social Housing Delivered via Housing Associations

There once existed a set of hybrid-type organisations which was originally intended to operate between the not-for-profit public sector and for-profit private sector called '*housing associations*'.

These organisations would take on the responsibilities of housing social tenants from local authorities and would be funded and regulated by the public sector (all whilst remaining a private entity). They were originally socially-minded private organisations that built and managed social housing properties for low-income communities.

But over the last decade, housing associations have had to evolve and adapt in order to survive the dramatic changes experienced in the UK housing market. Housing benefit cuts and numerous reductions in government funding have meant that housing associations have less capital to spend on building more low-rent social housing. These market pressures, coupled with the increased housing demand borne from the UK Housing Crisis, resulted in the reclassification of housing associations as '*private sector*' organisations. This shift allowed them to raise funds for house-building through issuing corporate bonds and participating in financial property markets.[21,22] This reclassification has ultimately changed the nature of housing associations, as they are now able to build full market value private housing for rent and sale to fill the funding gap created by withdrawn government funds.[23,24] Operating in the private sector also means that these organisations are susceptible to mergers and acquisitions, which further changes the nature of these organisations.

Following the current trajectory of change, modern-day housing associations are increasingly operating as commercially-minded landlords rather than the socially-minded landlord they were originally intended to be.

So, what does this all mean for the Mandem?

The public sector sees us as a financial burden and isn't in a financial position to take care of us. The private sector sees us as a poor investment and cuts corners in order to save on costs. And housing associations are being pressured into acting more and more like the private sector. All these components contributes to the gentrification of our spaces. And the Mandem end up as collateral. We must recognise that *privatisation* is an act of self-love. It's a form of self-defence. It affords us the ability to insulate the Ends from *market trends*.

And why should we remove ourselves from this turbulent system?

Because we are beautiful.

There's an unparalleled and unique beauty that exists in the Ends. This beauty exists because **we** occupy the space— it's our collective cultures, characters and identities that create this beauty

That being said, we shouldn't turn a blind eye to the troublesome activities that take place in the Ends. The baneful combination of road politics, over-policing, perceptions and prejudices drastically reduces our economic opportunities and quality of life. We need change. And in order to create change, we must harness the power of urban transformation, and transform the space(s) we occupy.

Many seek for positive change by having a change **of** environment, rather than changing **the** environment. The first solely benefits the self, the latter benefits the self *and* the collective within an environment (the non-zero sum game). Borrowing from a concept named the '*Right to the City*':

"The right to the city is ... [the] right to change ourselves by changing the city."

— **David Harvey, The Right to the City**[25] **(2008)**

The *Right to the City* was a concept first proposed by a French Marxist named Henri Lefebvre, in his 1968 book *Le Droit à la ville*.[26] He believed that the people should have the right to shape the city, and by transforming the city people would be able to transform themselves — for the better.

In essence, it's a socialist's response to the commodification of space driven by capitalism. Lefebvre understood the power that transformation of space has on a population, and called for control of urban spaces to be removed from capitalist entities ('*the private sector*') and into the hands of the people.[25,27]

Regardless of politics, the reality is that the space we occupy ('the Ends') operates under a capitalist system. The *Right to the City* is a noble idea, but to acheive this right is to abolish the commodification of land — which is a cornerstone of capitalism. Therefore to grant the right to shape the city to the people, is to abolish capitalism. And abolishing capitalism a demanding and impractical mission.[27]

Currently, the ability to change the city (or '*space*') is only reserved for those who possess ownership of the space. Our spaces ('*the Ends*') are under the ownership of either the public sector (local authority or housing association) or the private sector, and in both cases the ability to change the city is outsourced strictly to either of them.

If we can't change the city ('*the Ends*'), we can't change ourselves ('*the Mandem*') for the better. But... once we acquire ownership of our spaces, we inherit the ability to change the city ('*the Ends*') and can subsequently change ourselves. We are, after all, products of our environments — by owning our spaces, we afford ourselves the '*Right to **our** City*'.

Chapter Four

The Boatemah Way

Why aren't local authorities the only social housing landlord, and where did 'housing associations' come from?

Margaret Thatcher's Conservative government introduced the Housing Act of 1988 which prompted the creation of entities known as Housing Action Trusts (also known as HATs). HATs were created to repair and improve the living conditions of social housing estates across the country that suffering from major housing and social issues.[28] Once a HAT had completed the regeneration of a social housing estate, it would be transfer ed from local authority ownership to housing association ownership. The Conservative government's then-Environment Secretary, Nicholas Ridley, had refused tenants experiencing HAT regenerations, the right to vote on the transfer of the ownership of their homes.[29] The legitimacy of HAT developments were largely contested by members of parliament at the time,[30] and tenants had no say in the matter of who ran their homes.

In 1987, HATs had set their sights on the Angell Town estate in the London Borough of Lambeth. And at the time, the Angell Town community had suffered with poor housing conditions for a number of years, and were desperately yearning for improvement. The then-Environment Secretary denied the Angell Town community the right to vote on the HAT proposals,[30] thereby denying the community the ability to influence the tranformation of their urban space (denying them any Right to the City). Angell Town residents welcomed the redevelopment of their estate but wanted their voice to be heard— to influence the transformation of Angell Town more after their own hearts' desire. This denial did not bode well with Angell Town resident, **Dora Boatemah.**

Reluctant to concede community-control of Angell Town, Dora Boatemah set up the Angell Town Community Project (ATCP). She relentlessly campaigned for Angell Town's voting rights on the transfer of their homes. Mobilising the 2,000-strong Angell Town community to successfully vote against HAT intervention and fought a 10-year battle to ensure that Angell Town experienced a community-controlled redevelopment.[31,32]

"Don't bring us any more of your fancy designs. Ask us to brief you first... we have our own ideas."

— **Dora Boatemah, speaking to Planning Consultants**[33]

Despite political inertia and legislative obstructions, Dora's activism and ability to organise and form alliances with the residents of Angell Town allowed her community to be at the helm of Angell Town's redevelopment. She helped secure the tenancies of her community on the estate— something that would have otherwise not been guaranteed.[34]

"Angell Town people used to settle for anything, because anything was better than nothing. Now we insist on getting the very best possible."

— Dora Boatemah, Director of ATCP[35]

Dora was dubbed *"Difficult Dora"* due to her tenacity and fighting spirit. She may have been deemed difficult in the eyes of some— but in reality, she was a saint in the eyes of many others. Dora lobbied individuals from all walks of life and showed us that we're capable of rallying together in support of a common goal.

She fought to grant Angell Town the *Right to **their** City*.

Born July 22nd 1957 - died January 23rd 2001.

We Run

Chapter Five

the Block

As it currently stands, most of the Mandem are nothing more than tenants in these blocks. Even though we've invested more than most into our blocks and have lost more than most for our blocks, the Ends is not ours. But our sense of ownership over the Ends can be justified if we acquire legal ownership of the Ends.

To do that, we need to understand that there are two main types of property ownership:

Leasehold is the temporary ownership of a property over a predetermined duration.

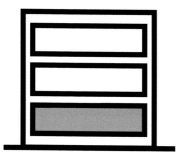

i.e. a property acquired under a lease (costs associated with a lease include ground rent, services charges and/or any other landlord charges).

Freehold is the absolute ownership of land or property.

i.e. a property owned outright. N.B. the "freeholder" is the legal owner of the freehold, also known as the "landlord".

The current landlords of our blocks (local authorities and/or housing associations) possess the freehold to the buildings that make up the Ends. In most cases, when attempting to purchase a flat in their building, tenants are only offered the option of purchasing a lease, where ownership of the property is temporary and reverts to the freeholder after the lease period has expired. The disadvantage of leasehold properties is that the building ultimately belongs to the freeholder, and leaseholders are liable to pay associated costs (such as ground rent and services charges). On top of this, leaseholders are not permitted to alter or improve the building they reside in without permission from the freeholder.

To own the Ends, is to own the freehold(s) of our buildings. Below is the blueprint to acquiring ownership of the Ends:

Legislation to use:

The Leasehold Reform Housing and Urban Development Act 1993

Name of process:

Collective Enfranchisement

Collective Enfranchisement is the right for leaseholders of a building to form a collective, and acquire the freehold of that building from the current freeholder.

Buildings only qualify for Collective Enfranchisement when:

- the building has no more than 25% non-residential use (e.g. shops, offices etc.)

  Note: garages in the building are classed as residential.

- at least two-thirds (66%) of the flats in the building are owned by qualifying tenants.

  Note: a qualifying tenant is a leaseholder whose lease is for a fixed term of more than 21 years. Tenants will not qualify if they own more than two flats in the building.

- the building must be a self-contained building, or part of a building, with at least two flats.

  N.B. if part of a building, there must be a vertical division of the building(s), with services either independent to that part, or could be so provided without significant interruption to the remaining part.

- the building is not within an Anglican cathedral precinct, a National Trust property, Crown property or where the freehold includes any operational railway, e.g. bridge tunnel, track.

Collective Enfranchisement is broken down into a four-phase process, the following pages takes you through this process.

Visit **page 83** for a summarised timeline of the overall process.

Phase 1:
ROUNDING UP THE MANDEM

The first phase of *Collective Enfranchisement* is as follows:

(i) Identify the Mandem & Sell the Idea of Ownership

Socialise the idea of privatisation; slide it into your conversations, write it into your music, bring it to life on film, and identify the changemakers on your block. This is a collective process that requires the support of the local community.

(ii) Incorporate the Mandem

In order for a building to qualify for *Collective Enfranchisement*, the residents of that building must actively campaign and gather support from their neighbours. At least half (50%) of qualifying tenants in a particular building must come together and form a *'Property Management Company'* (PMC). The PMC would be able to formally acquire the freehold of the building in question, and essentially become the *'new landlord'*.

A PMC may be registered as a company limited by shares, where the company could issue one share to every participating leaseholder. Each share would equate to a nominal value and every shareholder would be entitled to voting rights as a member of the company. Every organisation requires a director(s).

The leadership structure may be limited to a single director, but it's recommended that two or more directors take leadership of a PMC, as the position bears a lot of responsibility.

The appointment of a director occurs through 'resolution', a democratic voting process between all members of the PMC. The main responsibilities of a director include, but are not limited to:

- responsibilities to the members of the company
- responsibilities to the property

An 'Articles of Association' needs to be produced to communicate the purpose of the company and to govern voting rights and control of shares. The prescribed model of an Articles of Association can be found in the The Companies (Model Articles) Regulations 2008.

Solicitors specialising in Collective Enfranchisement or property law can support the production of the Articles of Association. These types of solicitors can be found via the Association of Leasehold Enfranchisement Practitioners (ALEP).

Phase 2:
PLOTTIN' THE MOVE

It's crucial that a PMC recruits a professionally accredited **building surveyor** and a **solicitor** to act on its behalf.

Not only are they able to provide general advice and counsel throughout the *Collective Enfranchisement* process, but their expertise is required to effectively deliver on the process. It's good practise to establish a *'fighting fund'* to cover the financial costs of surveying the building, the costs of information gathering, and the legal costs of a solicitor (and the costs of any potential tribunal proceedings).

(i) Bringing in the Solicitor & Collecting Information

As previously mentioned, the solicitor specialising in *Collective Enfranchisement* or property law can support the formal establishment of the PMC by producing an *Articles of Association* and divvying up control of shares. One of the solicitor's primary functions is to prepare the necessary information required to start the *Collective Enfranchisement* process. The information gathered by the solicitor includes:

- identity of the current freeholder(s) person or company name and address;

- full names and addresses of all leaseholders and details of their leases;

- details of any flats in the control of the freeholder.

Some of this information may already be available to the PMC. Information that is not freely available can be obtained through using legislation:

Landlord and Tenant Act 1985
it is your entitled right to obtain details of the name and address of your landlord. When requested, the information must be provided within 21 days. Failure to do so is an offence.

A potential hurdle is that the landlord of a building may not be the sole freeholder of the building, but one of a group of people/companies that share the freehold of the building. The solution to this would be to run a Land Registry search, or send an '*Information Notice*' to an identified landlord.

Land Registry
You are entitled to inspect the Land Register and obtain copies of the entry relating to the freehold in question. There's a small fee for copies of the register. The entry will provide the name and address of the registered owner(s) and details of any other interests in the freehold, including other freeholders.

Section 11 of the Leasehold Reform Regulations 1993 ('Information Notices')
Tenants have an entitled right to acquire information from the landlord, detailing any other freeholders or any intermediate leases, including the name and address of the lessee and the terms of the lease. The Information Notices can require sight of relevant documents (e.g. details of service charges or surveys). Recipients of the Notices are required to respond within 28 days.

N.B. Serving an Information Notice doesn't formally start the *Collective Enfranchisement* process or commit the tenants to the process in any way.

Acting as the representative of the PMC, solicitors will work in tandem with the building surveyor to respond to any landlord requests, challenges or counter-offers.

If the *Collective Enfranchisement* process succeeds, the solicitor conveys ('*transfers*') the property title from the previous landlord to the PMC, and amends the terms of existing leases of the building.

(ii) Bringing in the Surveyor & Assessing the Price

Building surveyors examine the existing condition of a building. In addition to identifying and analysing the structural condition (and its implications on future maintenance costs and/or service charges) of the building, a surveyor may draw up proposals for repair. Surveyors may advise on various building features such as:

- the energy efficiency of the building,
- preservation of historic buildings (Listed Buildings),
- management and maintenance of the building,
- health and safety concerns of the building.

It's highly recommended that the PMC commissions their surveyor to provide a preliminary valuation of the building in question. This would provide the PMC with a rough estimation of the final cost (and future associated costs) of the building before exercising the *Collective Enfranchisement* process. It's good practise to enlist the support of a '*chartered*' surveyor who is part of a professional membership body, such as the Royal Institution of Chartered Surveyors (RICS). These types of solicitors can be found on the RICS database.

Building surveyors calculate the 'highest and lowest' purchase price of a building's freehold through use of a formula cited in *Schedule 6, Part II of the Leasehold Reform Regulations act 1993*, along with their own professional judgement— valuing from both the perspectives of the leaseholders (newly-formed PMC) and the freeholder(s). There are a number of variables that affect the valuation of the freehold, such as:

The Ground Rent
This is a relatively small charge paid by leaseholders to the freeholder (e.g. annual charge of £100 to £500 per lease). If the freehold is to be purchased, the freeholder must be compensated for the loss of future ground rent earnings on leases that they've issued (inflation is also considered in the valuation).

Years Remaining on Lease(s)
'Freehold Reversion'
Ownership of a flat reverts to the freeholder once the duration of a lease has ended. If Collective Enfranchisement occurs, the anticipated reversion no longer happens, and the current freeholder loses their property. Therefore, the current freeholder must be compensated for the future loss of their property. This compensation is known as the 'Freehold Reversion'. The lower the number of years left on the lease, the higher the value of the 'Freehold Reversion'.

Value of the Flats
An assessment of the market value of each flat with their current leases (along with their value if the leases have a share of the freehold). The flats must be valued as if the right to Collective Enfranchisement (or the "Leasehold Reform Housing and Urban Development Act 1993") doesn't exist. Leaseholders participating in the freehold acquisition may be granted a discount against the value of flat if they have made any improvements to their property.

Marriage Value & Hope Value
In the case that there is less than 80 years remaining on a lease, the increase in the value of the flat caused by acquisition of the freehold must be shared 50:50 with the current freeholder. This is known as the 'Marriage Value'. There remains a hope that leased flats which don't participate in Collective Enfranchisement may request extensions on their lease in the future. The freeholder must be compensated for the loss of any future financial income from this hope; hence this is known as the 'Hope Value'. Generally, the Hope Value is much less and more flexible than the Marriage Value.

Additional costs that must be considered include title registration fees at the Land Registry, and Stamp Duty Land Tax (calculated as a fraction of the freehold price). Further expenses may be included for potential repairs and maintenance work to the building, which must also be factored into the overall costings.

Phase 3:
TAKING OVER

Once all the relevant information has been collated by both the appointed solicitor and building surveyor, the formal *Collective Enfranchisement* process may proceed.

(i) Serving the Section 13 Notice

The Section 13 Notice (also known as the '*Initial Notice*') is a formal notice sent to an existing freeholder which officially starts the Collective Enfranchisement process. The contents of the Initial Notice will be a compilation of information collected by the PMC's appointed solicitor and building surveyor, as well as a proposal on the purchase value and any other terms.

Once the PMC's solicitor serves the *Initial Notice* to the freeholder, the PMC becomes liable for the freeholder's legal costs from the date they receive the *Initial Notice*. Therefore the notice must contain no inaccuracies and must not be incomplete in order to avoid unnecessary expenses.

The required contents of the *Initial Notice* **are on the next page.**

Contents of the Section 13 Notice

Full names and addresses of:
- the freeholder(s) person or company name;
- all the qualifying tenants of the building and details of their leases;
- all the qualifying tenants submitting the Section 13 Notice;
- the Nominee Purchaser(s), in this case, the PMC.

Details of the flats and the premises you wish to acquire from the freeholder (complete with a plan and any relevant descriptions);

Rights inherited with acquisition of the freehold; e.g. vehicle access, rights of way, access to drainage, right to light, appurtenant property etc. (such matters must be described clearly and indicated using plan diagrams).

The grounds for Collective Enfranchisement claim; highlighting the eligibility of the claim; showcasing that the qualifications for *Collective Enfranchisement* are met, e.g. two-thirds of the flats in the building are owned by qualifying tenants, and the building is 75% residential use etc.

Details regarding any mandatory leasebacks; the current freeholder has the preserved right to mandatory leasebacks from the new freeholder. Therefore, the newly appointed freeholder is required to provide leasebacks of 'non-qualifying' flats to the social landlord (i.e. the local authority or the housing association). Mandatory leasebacks apply to flats: (i) let under a secure council tenancy, and (ii) let by housing associations under secure and assured tenancies. These leasebacks are charged at one peppercorn (£0.01) per annum ground rent on a 999-year lease.

Proposed purchase value of the freehold;

Date by when the Section 21 Notice must be served; Dated at least two months from the date of submission of Section 13 Notice, but no later than six months after.

Signatures of the Nominee Purchaser(s) and qualifying tenants.

(ii) Receiving the Section 21 Notice

The Section 21 Notice (also known as the 'Counter Notice') is subsequently served by the existing freeholder to the PMC, detailing their response to the *Initial Notice*. The *Counter Notice* outlines whether the freeholder:

- **accepts entitlement** to the freehold and the terms listed out in the notice (or provide alternative terms) or,

- **denies entitlement** to the freehold with justification (which can be assessed by a county court).

Additionally the *Counter Notice* may include other details such as:

Planned Redevelopment*
the freeholder may deny the sale of the freehold if there are plans for demolition and/or redevelopment of the building (either partially or the whole building).

> *N.B. the freeholder reserves this right, only when at least two thirds (66%) of the leases in the building are within **five years of termination** from the date that the Initial Notice is served.

Mandatory Leasebacks
the current freeholder has the preserved right to mandatory leasebacks from the new freeholder. Therefore, the newly appointed freeholder is required to provide leasebacks of 'non-qualifying' flats to the social landlord (i.e. the local authority or the housing association). Mandatory leasebacks apply to flats: (i) let under a secure council tenancy, and (ii) let by housing associations under secure and assured tenancies. These leasebacks are charged at one peppercorn (£0.01) per annum ground rent on a 999-year lease.

If the existing freeholder accepts the entitlement to the freehold on the Section 13 Notice, but disputes the terms laid out on the notice, such as the proposed purchase value of the freehold, both parties have two months to negotiate terms.

In the event that terms aren't agreed, then either party may apply for a First Tier Tribunal (aka 'Property Chamber') to rule on the terms.

Following application for a First Tier Tribunal, both parties have an additional four months to negotiate terms before a Tribunal hearing proceeds. In the scenario that a Tribunal hearing proceeds, the Tribunal would hear evidence from both parties—usually in the form of valuation evidence from each party's respective building surveyors.

Following the presentation of evidence, the Tribunal may be able to make a ruling and the parties may be able to enter into a legally binding contract. Each party is liable to pay their own legal costs of a First Tier Tribunal proceedings.

Phase 4:
CLEANIN' UP

When the *Collective Enfranchisement* process is completed, the freehold of the building is then transferred into the ownership of the PMC.

In the scenario that mandatory leasebacks of non-qualifying flats has taken place, the former freeholder is granted a lease(s) of these flats for a term of 999-years at a peppercorn ground rent. In essence, the former freeholder becomes a tenant of the new freeholder, and sub-leases the flat to their own tenants. Even at peppercorn ground rent, the lease granted is still subject to service charges, which would help cover the costs of maintenance and repairs of the building, and costs of insurance policies taken out for the building.

✓ The advantage of mandatory leasebacks is that the PMC benefits from an overall purchase price reduction due the exclusion of costs of non-qualifying flats. When compared to the cost of a flat in a building, the cost of the common areas (spaces between 'flats'/'dwellings' e.g. corridors, staircases etc.) of a building may not be as significant. Every qualifying flat increases the total cost of the freehold by hundreds of thousands of pounds. By avoiding the costs of purchasing every single flat in the building, the cost of acquiring the freehold may be dramatically reduced.

✗ The disadvantage of mandatory leasebacks is that the previous freeholder becomes a leasehold tenant on a 999-year lease, where social tenants have the flat(s) sublet to them, and the leaseholder acts as their sub-landlord.

Should there be mandatory leasebacks, legislation exists which allows tenants living in these flats to purchase the lease owned by their sub-landlord. Purchasing the lease allows the tenants to join and incorporate into the existing PMC, thereby eventually creating a building that is wholly owned by the tenants living in that building.

(i) Buying back the leasebacks

If the lease is owned by a **local authority**.

Legislation to use

The Housing Act 1985

Name of process

Right to Buy

Derived from Schedule 5 of the Housing Act 1985:

*"The right to buy does not arise unless the landlord owns the freehold or has an interest sufficient to grant a lease in pursuance of this Part for—
(a) ...
(b) where the dwelling-house is a flat, a term of not less than 50 years,
commencing, in either case, with the date on which the tenant's notice claiming to exercise the right to buy is served."*

Meaning: where the property is a flat, if the authority does not own the freehold of the block, the council tenant has the right to buy the leasehold only if the landlord is able to grant a lease of over 50 years.

If the lease is owned by a **housing association**.

Legislation to use

The Housing Act 1996

Name of process

Right to Acquire

Derived from Schedule 5 of the Housing Regulations 1997:

*"The right to acquire does not arise unless the landlord owns the freehold or has an interest sufficient to grant a lease in pursuance of this Part for—
(a) ...
(b) where the dwelling-house is a flat, a term of not less than 50 years,
commencing, in either case, with the date on which the tenant's notice claiming to exercise the right to acquire is served."*

Meaning: where the property is a flat, if the housing association does not own the freehold of the block, the housing association tenant has the right to acquire the leasehold only if the landlord is able to grant a lease of over 50 years.

By tenants exercising their right to obtain the leases of these flats, local authority and/or housing association leasehold ownership of a building can be phased out over time.

"Gentrify your own hood before these people do it. Claim eminent domain and have your people movin'."

— Shawn Carter, Jay-Z's B-Sides 2 show (2019)

Thugz

Chapter Six

Mansion

Picture it. Every building in the Ends owned by a unique property management company (PMC). A mosaic of blocks owned by the Mandem — complete sovereignty. And with sovereignty, we inherit the control of services and functions of our spaces which can lead to an unquantifiable amount of change.

"The social needs of a community should inform its economic agenda."

— George the Poet, "Have You Heard George's Podcast?" (2019)

The status quo has the talented members of our community providing services to people and places outside the Ends. The lack of space to accommodate this talent has had them relocating to spaces away from the Ends. Acquiring sovereignty in the Ends would afford the Mandem the ability to address *our* needs. We could create the space to accommodate *our* home-grown talent, bringing the Mandem back home to serve the Ends, and insourcing *our* talent to meet *our* own needs. Our needs would create demand for the Mandem to upskill in law, construction, design, security, finance, politics etc. By serving *ourselves*, we keep currency circulating within the Ends.

Possessing the freehold to the Ends creates new areas of opportunities for the Mandem, such as:

REVENUE &
VENTURE

There are a multitude of ventures that may take place when the freehold of a building is acquired. Examples include the construction of additional storeys to a block of flats, thereby increasing the number of residential units within the building and increasing the vertical height of the building.

Another example of venture is the conversion of ground floor residential units into commerical units. These in turn may be leased or rented out to business occupants such as retail, food and beverage businesses. Alternatively, a PMC may decide to lease out a commerical unit to non-traditional occupants such as science labs, AV production studios, performing arts studios, cinemas, leisure facilities etc. Matching the use of spaces in the Ends with the talent and character of the Mandem.

The creation of new residential units has the capacity to generate income via rent and service charge collection.

N.B. it's highly discouraged for members of the PMC to allow the subletting of their flats out to private tenants to generate rental income. Alternative revenue streams where the talents of the Mandem are utilised is more rewarding and creates greater value for the building, as well as the wider community.

M A I N T E N A N C E

The PMC would reserve the right to draw up their own contracts with businesses and tradesmen of their choice for the maintenance and upkeep of their building. Plumbers, electricians, cleaners, etc. may be contracted on the basis of their locality, expertise and relationship with the community.

The PMC would not only be able to decide who would be responsible for maintenance and upkeep, but when and how any work would take place.

Revenue streams would be cover the costs associated with building services such as:

- Repair works on the building structure
- Hygiene and aesthetic maintenance and/or improvements
- Insurance policies taken out on the building
- Management costs of running the building
- Utility (lighting, heating, cleaning) cost of common areas
- Costs of caretakers, receptionists and/or concierges

DESIGN&
RENOVATION

Landlords reserve the right to redesign and renovate a building under their possession. Examples of renovation works include:

Cosmetic improvements such as repainting and replastering walls, installing new flooring, changing a series of light fixtures etc. (any work that improves spaces in a building without affecting its structural integrity).

Or, **structural improvements** such as installing new double-glazed windows in each flat, rewiring electrics, replumbing bathrooms, knocking down interior walls, extensions of parts of the building, removal of flammable cladding on block façade etc.

E S T A T E
M A N A G E M E N T

Once a series of buildings are owned and managed by a group, it becomes the responsibility of the group to maintain the upkeep of the place their buildings occupy. Management activities are ultimately dictated by the needs of the community, but can be generally categorised under:

Security of the space and safety of its residents. As owners of space, it's possible that freeholders may decide to hire a private security detail committed to ensuring the safety of stakeholders in and around the buildings that they own. In the context of the Ends, the concept of a security detail patrolling a particular space isn't necessarily foreign. Freeholders may potentially be able to put the Mandem who already patrol the Ends for free, on a payroll.

Formalising the voice, image and identity of a space by creating an in-house marketing and PR team. Similar to the practise adopted by private developers, freeholders would be able to commission logos and colour palettes that speak to the shared identity of the local community. This form of imagery can rally the community together by creating impactful representations of the people, values, rules and/or history of the Ends. Practises such as monthly newsletters, social media accounts, public art displays are some of the ways that a landlord is able to showcase a neighbourhood's identity and culture.

Ensuring the functionality and safety of the building(s).
It is good practise to assemble an in-house safety, health, environment and quality (SHEQ) team to ensure that the premises are safe to live and work in.

Asset managing non-residential units of buildings. A leasing team would be essential if a number of a businesses occupy non-residential units. Functions would include rent collection, fit-outs, safety checks etc.

Bookkeeping of income, expenditure and transactions is essential. An in-house accountancy and legal counsel team can ensure that bookkeeping is happening, legal contracts are being adhered to, and that all stakeholder organisations are operating within the law.

Adjacent is a general organigram highlighting areas of management that a landlord would allocate resources to. The *'Executive Committee'* represents the freeholder(s)— this may be a single property management company, or a group of property management companies operating under an umbrella organisation, and the lines of reporting all feed into this committee for decision-making. The number of individuals running a specific area of management will vary between different landlords.

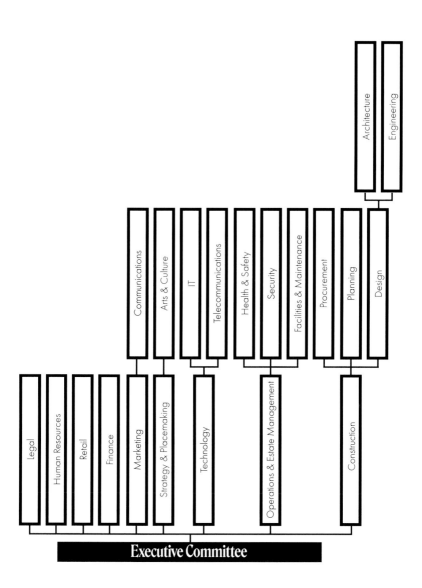

Executive Committee

Legal

Human Resources

Retail

Finance

Marketing

Strategy & Placemaking

Communications

Arts & Culture

IT

Telecommunications

Technology

Health & Safety

Security

Facilities & Maintenance

Operations & Estate Management

Procurement

Planning

Design

Construction

Architecture

Engineering

E X P A N S I O N

The Ends are made up of a collection of blocks situated in a single geographical location. In the scenario that Collective Enfranchisement has occurred across a whole estate, numerous PMCs may exist across the estate. PMCs may be unionised under a single 'umbrella organisation', where the umbrella organisation acts as the sole shareholder of the numerous PMCs across a single estate.

The advantages of this include the ability to share capital and revenue generated across different buildings on an estate, which would allow high income generators to support PMCs that may be dealing with a period of low income generation. Another advantage is the shared identity that comes with being under an umbrella organisation. Although the PMCs are separate, by assembling under one unified identity, they play to the strength of being part of a wider community.

These umbrella entities may have the capability to grow and extend outside of the boundaries of the Ends. With a portfolio of properties under their possession, access to finances may become available to umbrella entities (e.g. through borrowing against existing buildings, equity release loans etc.), providing them with access to capital which would enable them to acquire new land and expand the boundaries of the Ends.

Adhering to the following business model:

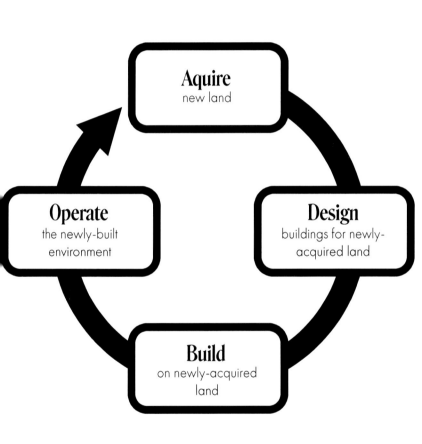

Aquire
new land

Design
buildings for newly-acquired land

Build
on newly-acquired land

Operate
the newly-built environment

Ownership allows us to change the Ends from a perceived space of destitution, indignity and crime, into a fully functioning city. A hub that retains its talent and creates opportunities for its future generations. Ownership allows us to change our cities, and changing our city allows us to change ourselves.

In 1943, psychologist Abraham Maslow famously developed a model for human motivation called the 'hierarchy of needs'.[36] As you ascend the hierarchy, the needs become less materialistic and more emotional. In this hierarchy of needs, the lower order areas (safety, food, shelter etc.) need to be fulfilled before the higher order areas (love, self-actualisation or 'purpose') can be achieved.

Owning our spaces allows us to have better control of the lower order areas ('basic needs') of the hierarchy. And solidifying the foundations of the hierarchy of needs allows the Mandem to achieve the higher order areas ('psychological needs' and purpose).

Purpose

Esteem
respect, status, confidence

Love
friendship, intimacy, family

Safety
security, employment, health

Physiological
food, water, sex, sleep, shelter

Psychological needs

Basics needs

Epilogue

Disclaimer: we will die before we see the fruits of our labour.

The Mandem must make peace with the reality that the privatisation of our communities will not happen in our lifetime. Privatising the Mandem isn't achievable within the next decade or two, it's a plan for the next century or two. If you want to create real long-term change, your long-term plans must outlive you.

By utilising the three forms of power:
> (i) the ability to 'influence';
> (ii) the generation of 'capital'; and,
> (iii) the acquisition of 'property';

our lineage will live in abundance, removed from dependency.

One day there'll be new rules, new regulations and new laws, rendering this document futile. When that day comes, I pray that this acts as a reminder of our tenacity and commitment to our communities.

"I'm not saying I'm gunna rule the world or I'm gunna change the world, but I guarantee you that I will spark the brain that will change the world. And that's our job, it's to spark somebody else watching us..."

— Tupac Amaru Shakur, MTV Interview (1994)

Afterword

On the Question of Privatising the Ends

Gerard Winstanley, the leader of the 1649 Diggers movement, once passionately declared that the Earth should serve as a *"common treasury for all"*. The Diggers were agrarian socialists who vehemently opposed the enclosure of land, which involved erecting physical barriers like walls, hedges, or fences around previously common land. Common land refers to land that is not under the ownership of a state (government, authority or council), or the market (private sector organisations or private citizens);[37] but one that is self-managed by a collective of individuals, known as commoners.

In the mid-1600s, commoners were deprived of their access to land that had previously been communal, along with all the natural resources it held. Access was now restricted exclusively to landowners and those they granted permission to.[38,39] The Diggers adamantly resisted the privatization of land and the transformation of shared resources into commodities. They called for the abolition of property ownership and disrupted the newly enclosed areas by engaging in practices such as land-squatting and planting their own crops on recently enclosed land.[40]

Fast forward several centuries, and the act of staking claim to land has become strongly encouraged. Culturally, the acquisition of land and property is perceived as a symbol of success. Economically, the market assigns exponential value to land, categorising properties as highly lucrative capital assets within the realm of global financial capitalism.[41]

In the contemporary landscape, we find the Abahlali baseMjondolo movement, founded in South Africa in 2005, employing tactics reminiscent of the Diggers. They utilise methods such as land occupations, protests, and disruptions of transportation networks to address housing and land-related issues in Durban.[42] The movement's core mission revolves around emphasising the social significance of land over its mere commercial value. In fact, both movements share the fundamental belief that land cannot be claimed by human beings, as it is inherently owned by a higher power. A representative from the Abahlali baseMjondolo movement once eloquently stated...[42]

"It is a sin for anyone to own land. Land comes from God and it cannot be owned"

It is crucial to recognize that the concept of land ownership, as understood in modern society today, was non-existent in pre-colonial South Africa. This is not to suggest that individuals had unrestricted freedom to roam without adhering to any social norms or decorum. Instead, the relationship between humans and land had a different character. Pre-colonial South African communities did not follow the conventional hierarchical system where '*landowners*' held exclusive rights and interests over a particular space.

Instead, emphasis was placed on the obligations people had toward a particular space, **in relation to** others who also occupied that space. Individuals were granted temporary rights to utilise resources in a given area only during the time of their utilisation, rather than asserting ultimate ownership over the property.[42]

The shift of early humans from nomadic lifestyles to settler lifestyles had a profound impact on the commodification of common resources. As settlers established their presence on a piece of land, they automatically asserted exclusive *'rights over the property,'* effectively excluding others from accessing the resources within that land. This exclusivity led to a reduced overall supply of resources available to the broader community. This scarcity, in turn, provided an economic advantage to these *'landowners'* over others.[43] The process of commodifying land and property, through actions like colonisation and the establishment of settlements on new territories, ultimately led to the demise of the commons. Consequently, land that remains unclaimed by humans has become a rare phenomenon.

This reality is exemplified in England, as emphasized in Guy Shrubsole's book, *"Who Owns England?"* In England, the majority of land is owned either by the state (public sector, including the Crown) or the market (private sector organizations or individuals). However, an intriguing aspect arises in the form of the *'unaccounted for'* 17% of land, seemingly devoid of any owner.

Percentage of Landownership in England

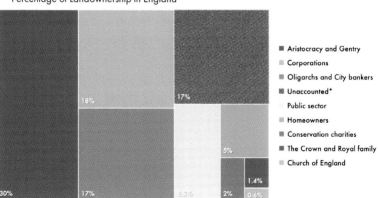

Shrubsole suspects that this unaccounted for land* is, in fact, under the ownership of long-standing aristocratic families who have not formally registered their claims at the Land Registry, as these estates have been inherited for centuries, long before the establishment of the Land Registry in 1862.

In his 1968 book "*Le Droit à la ville*", French Marxist Henri Lefebvre, describes the transformative power that an urban space (the '*city*', along with its transformation) has on its inhabitants. He goes as far as to call for the control of urban spaces to be removed from the market and into the hands of the people – naming this concept, the *Right to the City*:

"The right to the city is [...] far more than a right of individual or group access to the resources that the city embodies: it is a right to change and reinvent the city more after our hearts' desire."

The right to transform urban areas was once held by commoners, where a collective right to land meant that the transformation of common land was shaped by its users. However, after centuries of enclosure and land appropriation, the modern landscape has become divided into parcels of land owned by both the state and the market, and it is now solely the landowners who possess the power to transform urban areas within their ownership.

It is essential to note that the nature of capitalism is the relentless pursuit of self-interest, as described by philosopher and economist Adam Smith:[45]

"It is not from the benevolence of the butcher, the brewer, or the baker, that we expect our dinner, but from their regard to their own interest."

For the market, the primary interest is generating surplus capital, and any urban changes within their domain are shaped by this interest.

In contrast, state-owned land is expected to prioritize the people's interests over profit. The state is theoretically bound by the Nolan Principles, a set of seven values upheld by all public servants and elected officials, emphasising "*selflessness*" as the first principle, defined as acting solely in the interests of the public.[46] Therefore, there is an assumption that a landowner bound by a principle of selflessness would not act in self-interest, thus providing its people with access to state-owned land and the resources it possesses.

But in practice, the state falls short of this ideal when exercising the transformative power it possesses over its claim. The source of the majority of these state failings is the subjective definition of the interests of the people.

In the context of New York, USA, notable state urban planner Robert Moses drastically transformed the city's infrastructure to prioritise motor vehicles while neglecting public transit systems like rail and bus services intentionally.

He believed that the people's interests lay in traversing America in motor vehicles and thus designed and constructed approximately 627 miles of motorways within the city. However, this design approach effectively excluded non-motor vehicle forms of transit, driven by Moses's racial and class biases. Consequently, it marginalised a significant portion of the population reliant on public transportation.[49]

Moses held biases against the 'slum' areas of New York and cleared these areas to make space for expressways, viewing the demolished spaces and their inhabitants as collateral damage in the interest of the people he served. The damage caused by his actions has been documented through photography taken at the time, with countless images capturing the trenches cutting through the Bronx in the 1980s for the Cross Bronx Expressway, displacing approximately 1,500 families.

(Figure 1)

(Figure 2)

Robert Moses serves as a testament of the detrimental impact of state-driven urban transformation when not aligned with the interests of the communities it serves.

In modern-day London, the failures of state-sponsored urban transformation are evident in the gentrification of various city areas. Gentrification, a term coined by Ruth Glass in the 1960s and popularised by Professor Loretta Lees, refers to:[51]

"The transformation of a working-class or vacant area of the central city to a middle class residential and/or commercial use."

Gentrification often targets working-class neighborhoods, particularly social housing estates known as the Ends. These estates, typically owned by public sector entities and supported by state welfare, are frequently earmarked for regeneration by state municipalities. This process mirrors the urban renewal initiatives carried out in the Bronx under Robert Moses and is driven by various factors, including economic pressures.

The 2010 UK General Election led to the formation of a Conservative and Liberal Democrat coalition government, which initiated a decade-long series of austerity measures across the nation. These measures resulted in significant budget cuts to housing, health, policing, and public services, reducing local authority resources. Simultaneously, a chronic housing supply shortage failed to meet demand, compelling the state to undertake social housing estate regeneration, often against the interests of the people.

So, why is the regeneration of London's social housing estates not in the people's interest?

In essence, such regeneration schemes do not meet the people's needs but rather displace them. The net loss of social tenure homes during estate regeneration projects stems from various economic constraints faced by the state. Many of these proposals are joint ventures with private sector organizations, known as public-private partnerships (PPPs),[56,57] as the state alone cannot deliver on the housing supply needed to meet the market's demand. As private sector organizations' primary interest is in gaining the highest possible return on investment - this is acheived by tinfluencing state policies and lobbying for regeneration projects. As a result, the boundary between the state and the market becomes increasingly blurred.

So, what about privatising the 'Ends'?

Allowing communities residing in social housing estates to gain ownership of their living spaces would transfer the power of urban transformation from the state into the hands of the people. As David Harvey expresses in his 2013 book "Rebel Cities":

"... through the exercise of private property rights, [...] when [...] collectively buy a building [a space can] be used for some progressive purpose. [...] they can establish a commune or a soviet within some protected space."

If the Mandem are able to acquire ownership of their urban spaces, and collectively agree to a new way of governing their spaces (one focused on collective interests rather than individual self-interest) – privatisation has the potential to shape a new type of city.

One that is shaped by the Mandem.

Appendix

Percentage of Building owned

Detailed Breakdown of Collective Enfranchisement

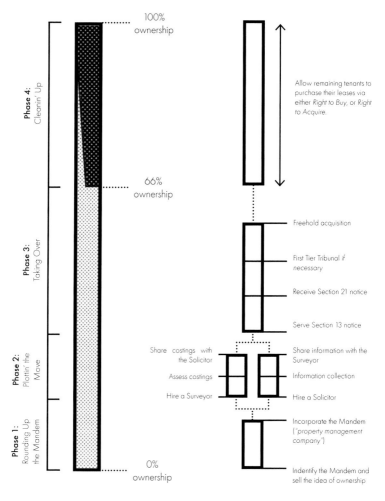

100% ownership

66% ownership

0% ownership

Phase 4: Cleanin' Up

Phase 3: Taking Over

Phase 2: Plottin' the Move

Phase 1: Rounding Up the Mandem

Allow remaining tenants to purchase their leases via either *Right to Buy*, or *Right to Acquire*.

Freehold acquisition

First Tier Tribunal *if necessary*

Receive Section 21 notice

Serve Section 13 notice

Share costings with the Solicitor

Assess costings

Hire a Surveyor

Share information with the Surveyor

Information collection

Hire a Solicitor

Incorporate the Mandem (*"property management company"*)

Indentify the Mandem and sell the idea of ownership

Bibliography

1. Singleton J. *Boyz n the Hood*. Columbia Pictures; 1991.

2. Meuller B. What Is Austerity and How Has It Affected British Society? The New York Times. Published February 24, 2019. Accessed February 11, 2021. https://www.nytimes.com/2019/02/24/world/europe/britain-austerity-may-budget.html

3. Local Government Association. Local government funding: Moving the conversation on. Published online July 3, 2018:12. Accessed February 11, 2021. https://www.local.gov.uk/moving-the-conversation-on/funding

4. Maguire P, Chakelian A. The deepest cuts: austerity measured. *New Statesman*. Published online October 10, 2018. Accessed March 15, 2021. https://www.newstatesman.com/politics/uk/2018/10/deepest-cuts-austerity-measured

5. Oxfam. *The Trust Cost of Austerity and Inequality*.; 2013. Accessed March 9, 2021. www.oxfam.org

6. Affordable Housing Commission. *Why Is Housing Unaffordable ? A Literature Review for the Affordable Housing Commission*.; 2019. Accessed February 11, 2021. www.affordablehousingcommission.org

7. Savage M. Social housing is a vanishing option for families who cannot afford to buy. *The Guardian*. https://www.theguardian.com/society/2018/jun/24/social-housing-no-longer-option-young-families. Published June 24, 2018. Accessed March 16, 2021.

8. Stothart C. UK grant-funded completions drop by half as new AHP gets started. *Social Housing*. https://www.socialhousing.co.uk/insight/insight/uk-grant-funded-completions-drop-by-half-as-new-ahp-gets-started-26460. Published November 3, 2016. Accessed February 11, 2021.

9. Wainwright O. Meet the councils quietly building a housing revolution. *The Guardian*. https://www.theguardian.com/cities/2019/oct/28/meet-the-councils-quietly-building-a-housing-revolution. Published October 28, 2019. Accessed February 11, 2021.

10. Butler P. Government accused of wrecking plans to build more social housing. The Guardian. https://www.theguardian.com/society/2019/oct/11/government-accused-wrecking-plans-build-more-social-housing?CMP=share_btn_tw. Published October 11, 2019. Accessed February 11, 2021.

11. Wainwright O. Revealed: how developers exploit flawed planning system to minimise affordable housing. *The Guardian*. https://www.theguardian.com/cities/2015/jun/25/london-developers-viability-planning-affordable-social-housing-regeneration-oliver-wainwright. Published June 25, 2015. Accessed February 11, 2021.

12. Bartholomew E. Why is award-winning Hoxton council block Bridport House still defective seven years on? *Hackney Gazette*. https://www.hackneygazette.co.uk/news/hoxton-council-block-bridport-house-undergoes-brickwork-tests-3603398. Published August 30, 2018. Accessed February 11, 2021.

13. Raffray N. "Defective" L&Q homes in South Kilburn slammed by flat owners and tenants as service charges rocket. *Brent & Kilburn Times*. https://www.kilburntimes.co.uk/news/l-q-homes-in-south-kilburn-slammed-3816940. Published May 17, 2019. Accessed February 11, 2021.

14. BBC News. Ministers pledge to end "poor doors" in new build housing. bbc.co.uk. Published July 19, 2019. Accessed February 11, 2021. https://www.bbc.co.uk/news/uk-49053920

15. Grant H, Michael C. Too poor to play: children in social housing blocked from communal playground. *The Guardian.* https://www.theguardian.com/cities/2019/mar/25/too-poor-to-play-children-in-social-housing-blocked-from-communal-playground. Published March 25, 2019. Accessed February 11, 2021.

16. Wainwright O. Penthouses and poor doors: how Europe's "biggest regeneration project" fell flat. *The Guardian.* https://www.theguardian.com/artanddesign/2021/feb/02/penthouses-poor-doors-nine-elms-battersea-london-luxury-housing-development. Published February 2, 2021. Accessed February 11, 2021.

17. Booth R. Social housing funding system is "nuts", says top property developer. *The Guardian.* https://www.theguardian.com/society/2018/may/14/social-housing-funding-system-is-nuts-says-top-property-developer. Published May 14, 2018. Accessed February 11, 2021.

18. Perry J. Is this the end of Section 106? Inside Housing. https://www.insidehousing.co.uk/comment/comment/is-this-the-end-of-section-106-67449. Published August 10, 2020. Accessed February 11, 2021.

19. Apps P. The end of Section 106 could prove a transformative moment for affordable housing. *Inside Housing.* https://www.insidehousing.co.uk/comment/comment/the-end-of-section-106-could-prove-a-transformative-moment-for-affordable-housing-67414. Published August 5, 2020. Accessed February 11, 2021.

20. Backhaus J. Is this really the end for section 106? *Constr Manag.* Published online January 7, 2021. Accessed March 10, 2021. https://constructionmanagermagazine.com/is-this-really-the-end-for-section-106/

21. Stothart C. Housing associations returned to private sector. *Social Housing.* https://www.socialhousing.co.uk/news/news/housing-associations-returned-to-private-sector-53260. Published November 16, 2017. Accessed March 14, 2021.

22. Public Sector Executive. Housing associations classified as private in bid to fix market's 'many faults.' *Public Sector Executive.* https://www.publicsectorexecutive.com/Public-Sector-News/housing-associations-classified-as-private-in-bid-to-fix-markets-many-faults. Published November 16, 2017.

23. Smyth S. The future of housing associations in England: commercially minded, commercially hearted. *LSE BPP.* Published online March 5, 2020. Accessed February 11, 2021. https://blogs.lse.ac.uk/politicsandpolicy/housing-associations-commercialisation/

24. Scanlon K, Whitehead C, Blanc F. *The Future Social Housing Provider.*; 2017.

25. Harvey D. David Harvey, The Right to the City, NLR 53, September–October 2008. New Left Review. Published September 2018. Accessed February 12, 2021. https://newleftreview.org/issues/ii53/articles/david-harvey-the-right-to-the-city

26. Lefebvre H. Le droit à la ville. *L Homme la société.* 1967;6(1):29-35. doi:10.3406/homso.1967.1063

27. Frantzanas S. The right to the city as an anti-capitalist struggle. *ephemera.* 2014;14(4). Accessed February 24, 2021. www.ephemerajournal.org

28. Rao N. The Changing Role of Local Housing Authorities. An Interim Assessment. Published

online 1990. Accessed February 11, 2021. http://www.psi.org.uk/publications/publication.asp?publication_id=24

29. Fraser R. Dora Boatemah. *The Guardian*. https://www.theguardian.com/news/2001/feb/06/guardianobituaries. Published February 6, 2001. Accessed February 11, 2021.

30. House of Commons. Housing Action Trusts. Housing Action Trust Areas. Published November 11, 1988. Accessed February 11, 2021. https://hansard.parliament.uk/commons/1988-11-11/debates/b537d61e-86d6-4727-a59d-c45d4492fee7/HousingActionTrustAreas

31. Worsley G. One woman's dream of decent homes. *The Telegraph*. https://www.telegraph.co.uk/finance/property/new-homes/4814778/One-womans-dream-of-decent-homes.html. Published December 31, 2001. Accessed February 11, 2021.

32. Sheeran L. Daring in the community. *The Guardian*. https://www.newspapers.com/clip/58935626/daring-in-the-community/. Published September 21, 1994. Accessed February 11, 2021.

33. Blair T. How to tackle the London social housing crisis? Chronicle World. Published March 11, 2016. Accessed March 15, 2021. https://chronicleworld.net/2016/03/11/how-to-tackle-the-social-housing-crisis/

34. Akingbade A. *Street* 66.; 2018. Accessed February 11, 2021. http://film-directory.britishcouncil.org/street-66

35. Burrell Foley Fischer LLP. Angell Town — Burrell Foley Fischer LLP. Accessed March 15, 2021. https://bff-architects.com/angell-town-residential

36. Maslow AH. A theory of human motivation. *Psychol Rev*. 1943;50(4):370-396. doi:10.1037/h0054346

37. Hardin G. The Tragedy of the Commons. Science (1979). 1968;162(3859):1243-1248. http://www.jstor.org/stable/1724745

38. Mingay GE. Parliamentary Enclosure in England: An Introduction to Its Causes, Incidence, and Impact, 1750-1850. Longman; 1997. https://books.google.co.uk/books?id=Lf3sAAAAMAAJ

39. Short C. The traditional commons of England and Wales in the twenty-first century: meeting new and old challenges. International Journal of the Commons. 2008;2(2):192. doi:10.18352/ijc.47

40. Gurney J. Gerrard Winstanley's : Context and Continuity. In: Ramiro Avilés MA, Davis JC, eds. Utopian Moments : Reading Utopian Texts. 1st ed. Textual Moments in the History of Political Thought. Bloomsbury Academic; 2012:47-52. http://www.bloomsburycollections.com/book/utopian-moments-reading-utopian-texts/ch8-gerrard-winstanley-s/

41. Ward J, Greenwood L. Land Value Growth in UK Hotspots.; 2015. Accessed June 8, 2022. https://www.savills.co.uk/research_articles/229130/186381-0

42. Pithouse R. An Urban commons? Notes from South Africa. Community Development Journal. 2014;49(suppl_1):i31-i43. doi:10.1093/cdj/bsu013

43. du Plessis E. African Indigenous Land Rights in a Private Ownership Paradigm. Potchefstroom Electronic Law Journal/Potchefstroomse Elektroniese Regsblad. 2011;14. doi:10.4314/pelj.v14i7.3

44. Harvey D. Rebel Cities: From the Right to the City to the Urban Revolution. Verso; 2013.

45. Smith A. The Wealth of Nations / Adam Smith ; Introduction by Robert Reich ; Edited, with Notes, Marginal Summary, and Enlarged Index by Edwin Cannan. New York : Modern Library, 2000.; 1776. https://search.library.wisc.edu/catalog/999905503902121

46. Spicker P. Seven Principles of Public Life: time to rethink. Public Money & Management. 2014;34(1):11-18. doi:10.1080/09540962.2014.865927

47. Caro RA. The Power Broker : Robert Moses and the Fall of New York. [First edition]. New York : Knopf, 1974.; 1974. https://search.library.wisc.edu/catalog/999476860402121

48. Ploschnitzki P. Robert Moses, the Construction of the Cross Bronx Expressway and its impact on the Bronx. University of Arizona. Published online 2017.

49. Burns R. New York: A Documentary Film. PBS; 2003.

50. Sedensky M. NEIGHBORHOOD REPORT: BRONX UP CLOSE; Decades Later, Doing the Cross Bronx Expressway Right. The New York Times. October 7, 2001.

51. Lees L. Gentrification / Loretta Lees, Tom Slater, Elvin Wyly. (Slater T, Wyly EK, eds.). Routledge; 2007. http://www.loc.gov/catdir/toc/ecip077/2006103339.html

52. Cheshire J, Hall D, Adger D. Multicultural London English and social and educational policies. Languages, Society & Policy. Published online May 21, 2017.

53. Cheshire J, Kerswill P, Fox S, Torgersen E. Contact, the feature pool and the speech community: The emergence of Multicultural London English. Journal of Sociolinguistics. 2011;15(2):151-196. doi:10.1111/j.1467-9841.2011.00478.x

54. Khan O. The Colour of Money: How Racial Inequalities Obstruct a Fair and Resilient Economy. Runnymede Trust. Published online 2020.

55. Gulliver K. Forty Years of Struggle: A Window on Race and Housing, Disadvantage and Exclusion. Human City Institute. Published online 2016.

56. Local Government Association. House of Commons debate – Role of developers, housebuilders, and management companies in new homes January 2022. Published online January 2, 2022.

57. Local Government Association. Public-Private Partnerships: Driving Growth, Building Resilience. Published online January 10, 2022.

Figure 1: Lehman College Library, CUNY. (Unknown) Cross Bronx Expressway Under Construction (2 of 2) [Photograph]. Place of publication: Bronx Chamber of Commerce Collection.

Figure 2: de Leon, P. (1980) My Playground [Photograph]. Place of publication: Smithsonian American Art Museum.

Designed by:

**FREEDOM
& BALANCE**